I0481913

First Money In

How to Raise your first $500, $5,000 or $50,000 for your business or idea

By Julien L. Meyer, MBA.

x

i

To all the entrepreneurs who struggle day in and day out to chase a dream

TABLE OF CONTENT

PART I

Foreword

I've wanted to write this book for quite some time, and now I have finally begun to do it. It's 12:18 pm on Wednesday, March 7, 2018. I went to a bookstore in Northvale, New Jersey, and purchased a small yellow moleskin notebook. It is in this book where I will write down my thoughts: a guide on what it takes for entrepreneurs to raise early-stage capital in today's world.

We live in a world dominated by social media and false information. As a three-time tech founder turned startup coach and venture capital consultant, a lot of what I see and hear about early stage venture capital is broken. The grit, tenacity, charisma, talent, and skill that entrepreneurs and founders need to succeed are just as important as that first money you put into a company or idea. We all know the classic saying, "It takes money to make money," and in many ways this statement could not be more relevant to the entrepreneur. However, as useful as funds are to a company and entrepreneurs, they can also be corruptive. Raise too much money and you will just spend it like a fool; raise too little, and you will spend all of your time fundraising thereby making you unable to compete. This problem comes in large part from the recent "tech startup" boom which has created a world full of overfunding and poor business practices.

I'm writing this book to beg for some common sense and to demonstrate how to raise the proper amount of money for a project and how easy it can be to secure your first round of capital, startup money, or founding money. I've been raising money for businesses my entire career, so it's fair to say that I've learned a few things along the way. Over the course of this book, you'll learn about creative ways to secure funds for an idea, business venture, or startup. My goal with this book is to help at least one entrepreneur discover new strategies to secure that initial money you need to start your company.

This book was inspired by Peter F. Drucker's classic management manual, *Managing Oneself*. Most books on fundraising and venture capital are hundreds of pages long and filled with dense, boring legal material. These books are very helpful when you're raising larger rounds of capital, for example, $250,000 or more, but my book is designed to be a pocket-sized guide to help you secure that first $500, $5,000, or $50,000 that you need to start your business and start chasing your dream.

Redefining Early Stage Capital

Venture capital, angel investors, pre-seed, seed, Series A, Series A2, Series B: These are just some of the common terms you hear when discussing fundraising for a business. If they sound confusing, that's because that's what they're designed to do. As someone who is now on the investing side of entrepreneurship, I can tell you firsthand that investors want you to be confused so that they can "educate you," "be smarter than you," and dictate their terms to you. They want to be perceived as the smartest people in the room because that's how they get the best deal for their investors. Furthermore, the narrative that they want you to believe is that when it comes to fundraising and starting a business, it's their way or the highway.

This simply is not true, especially when raising $250,000 or less. See, the problem with early-stage capital (or your first round) is that if you just learn some basic tools and are informed of a few basic things, raising $500, $5,000, or even $50,000 becomes a joke and sometimes you don't even have to give up equity. After working with dozens of clients/startups, raising early-stage capital, and coaching hundreds of entrepreneurs on their fundraising efforts, I have found that even the best and brightest first-time founders don't know the tips and tricks necessary to effectively raise their first round of startup capital.

That brings us back to the purpose of this book. Remember, what you are going to learn throughout this book are a number of creative strategies to secure that very first $500, $5,000, or even $50,000, for your business venture or idea. If you've already raised funds or are looking for $1 million or more in first-round capital, this book may not be for you.

One of the biggest mistakes most of my first-time founder clients make is thinking they need to raise $300,000, $500,000 or even $1 million to get their idea to the next phase when really this is just BS. They have made this assumption based off of bloated quotes from developers, advice from business people (not experienced entrepreneurs), and based off a sheer lack of knowledge as to what tools and resources are available to them in the age of the Internet.

One of my clients was under the impression he needed to raise $300,000, and in a quick analysis we determined that he only needed $5,000 to get a prototype built and another $25,000 later on to get the first version of his software out. This isn't complicated stuff; it's just knowledge that has yet to be shared, which you are about to get now.

Your First Round of Funding: How Much Money Do You Really Need?

When you're a first-time founder, advice (good and bad) is going to come at you from every direction. Friends, family, colleagues, potential investors, potential team members, experienced entrepreneurs are all going to want to put their two cents in. I have this saying: good entrepreneurs know when to listen, but great entrepreneurs know when to ignore. What this means is that as a founder you have to be strong and realize that although there is plenty of good advice out there, if someone hasn't gone down your exact path, there's a good chance they don't know what they're talking about. Because of this fact, many first-time founders are ill informed on many topics, including capital requirements and fundraising. When you're a first-time founder or if you're in an early stage of your business venture, always be sure to vet the people who are giving you "advice."

So, how much capital do you actually need to get started? Did you go to a developer who said he/she would need $100,000 to build your app or website? Did you talk to a lawyer who said you would need $5,000 to work with them? Did a colleague or advisor say you would need $25,000 to get going? The point I am trying to illustrate is that everyone and anyone who helps you determine how much money you need to get started will have different ideas. Your first round of capital is unique and different than subsequent fundraising rounds. If you were my client, I would advise you to use the following formula to do a rough estimate as to how much capital you need to raise:

Monthly burn rate (exaggerated and all inclusive) x 18 months x 1.2 (growth capital) = approximate amount you should raise.

But this is not necessarily true for first-round capital. Most VCs and angel investors want you to believe that this is what you should be doing from day one because that is how they get the best deals and lowest valuation on your company.

Your goal with raising the very first money you need for your company or idea should be to cut as much BS out from your first budget and secure that amount to get going. Now, many Silicon Valley VCs are going to tell you that I'm wrong, but I don't give a damn. I am based in New York City's Silicon Alley, and we know a thing or two about finance over here. If you're plugged into Silicon Valley, a former Google employee, or a well-known entrepreneur, none of these rules apply. These entrepreneurs have the benefit of being able to secure massive amounts of capital just from a pitch deck in order to assemble the best teams immediately and quickly crush the competition and get acquired in 12 to 48 months.

For the other 99.9% of entrepreneurs though, this model and narrative of raising as much money as you can early on can be quite toxic and corrosive. The goal with your first round of capital is to raise that $500, $5,000, or $50,000, and to take your idea from... well, just that: an idea into a business.

Here's how you determine how much capital you need to get going at this stage:

1) What are the five most important things you need to spend money on to get this idea going? (Lawyers, team members, Web design, etc.)

a)_____

b)_____

c)_____

d)_____

e)_____

2) Re-visit question one and assign rough estimate dollar amounts to the right of each item:

a)_____

b)_____

c)_____

d)_____

e)_____

3) Revisit question one and cross out three of the five options:

a)_____

b)_____

4) Add the remaining two dollar amounts and write that number below:

a)_____

b)_____

5) Write down the new total below:

$_____

Crazy simple, right? Think I'm oversimplifying it? I promise you I'm not. The biggest idea/startup killer is not getting started. It's daunting and difficult to raise $500,000 or more, and the thought of that alone scares off enough people that they simply repress their dreams.

Did you come up with a number between $500 and $50,000 in the section before? If you did, good job. If you didn't, no problem. Over the next sections I will have you revisit everything you wrote down and you'll have the opportunity to perform a slightly modified version of that same exercise.

How much capital do you really need?

In the previous section we used a rough exercise to determine how much money you might need to get your idea off the ground. Now, we're going to discuss some strategies to figure out how much you really need, and then, once we've done that, the rest of this book will be dedicated to actually helping you secure that capital.

So, how much money do you really need to get started? Remember, the goal here is to secure the minimum amount of capital to transform your idea into a business. This is super important for two reasons. By allocating the minimum amount of money necessary for a new idea, you minimize your risk and the initial valuation of your company will increase (unless you are one of the .01% of well known, ex-Google, Stanford SV entrepreneurs). Doing so will also teach you to be scrappy and fiscally responsible, which are two of the most important skills entrepreneurs can develop.

What were your most important costs in the previous section? Website development? App development, legal fees, market research, team members? We will address each one of these in a moment with regard to strategies on how you can trim down those expenses, but first we will cover the general principle on how you can drastically reduce your startup costs.

How to save money?

First, it is important to remember that everything and anything can be negotiated! If you don't consider yourself a great negotiator, or just need to brush up on your negotiating skills, pick up a copy of *Never Split the Difference: Negotiating As If Your Life Depended On It* by Chris Voss. Second, you have to remember that the concept of capital OPM, or Other People's Money, is much more valuable than your own money. For more information on this, be sure to read Jay Samit's book, *Disrupt You!*

How have you determined your start up budget up until this point? Googled prices for app development? Spoke to experts on Web design? Called one lawyer? Entrepreneurs have to be scrappy. We have to turn over every rock to find people who will help us get started early on for free or at a very low cost. Simple tip: Did you already know this? How many developers have you called? How many lawyers have you spoken to? Have you offered to trade work in lieu of money paid for services rendered yet? Have you approached bored retirees, who still have a lot of talent to help you get started? Are you going to your local university's computer science clubs to find great talent at a low cost? (Some college kids will work just for a hot meal!)

These are the skills and strategies you need to deploy at this stage. What a "professional" graphic designer or developer will quote you, you can almost always get at $1/10^{th}$ the cost just by hustling and networking with younger or retired developers and designers. The same concept comes into play with lawyers and other business services you might need. Are you using http://www.meetup.com to network with business lawyers who almost always give a discount to startups (sometimes free services in exchange for future business)? Are you using your local WeWork office to network with other entrepreneurs and trade out services to help each other? This is the mindset you need to develop early on to truly determine how much startup capital you need. Employ some of these strategies now, and you will be surprised at how past quotes of $200,000 or $80,000 will seem exorbitant when some of these people will offer you the same services for $20,000 or $8,000 or even for free. Remember, the most important thing at this stage is to get your idea from an idea to a business. The less capital that needs to be laid out upfront, the more likely you will be to get started.

How to save money: Getting started, legal fees, and startup costs

Most first-time founders think that starting a business—incorporating it, rather—is some huge, difficult, and expensive task. This could not be further from the truth, especially here in the United States. When it comes to incorporation costs, licensing and insurance, you can get all of this set up in most states for under $1,000. Where this gets expensive is when you start to use services like Legal Zoom or overpriced lawyers who are merely middlemen. To avoid the pitfalls of spending too much on incorporating you need to follow these tips:

- Do the research on your state's department of business site to determine actual incorporation costs.

- Does it make sense to incorporate in a different state? Do the research.

- Use something like NOLO's guide on how to set up an LLC to get informed on different types of incorporation so that you don't get taken for a ride. (Link: http://www.nolo. com)

- Visit my free Udemy course called "How to Start a Startup" to see just how easy it is to incorporate. (Link: https://www.udemy. com/how-to-start-a-startup-business/)

Now, of course your best bet and my recommendation is to work with a great startup or business lawyer with expertise in your field. But didn't you just say to avoid lawyers? No. I said to avoid overpriced lawyers. Most first-time entrepreneurs call the first law firm they can find or go to a general local lawyer to incorporate their businesses. Not all lawyers are created equal. Not all law firms are created equal. The way to save money while still setting up your business the right way is not to cut out a lawyer altogether but to find a startup lawyer who will provide maximum value to you. As a matter of fact, the earlier you build a relationship with a great lawyer, the better off it will be for you. The trick to keeping your legal fees low is to find a lawyer who gives discounts to new business owners. Does this exist, you ask? Yes!

This is one of the best-kept secrets in entrepreneurship, and I didn't know this was possible until my third startup.

So how do you find one of these lawyers? Remember our general tips? Networking? Everything's negotiable! Same applies here. You have to put yourself out there. Get on http://www.meetup.com look for business mixers in and around your city, attend the events and spot the lawyers (usually dressed to the nines, with a slight shimmer in their eye). Start talking to these lawyers. Ask what their firm specializes in. Ask what they specialize in. You want to find a startup/entrepreneur/IP lawyer. When you find one, ask if they have discounts for new startup clients or deferred payment options. Tell them about your idea and if they like it, they will most likely offer you a preferred rate for a discount.

Another way to find these lawyers is to go to your local chamber of commerce and ask if they have relationships with any startup lawyers. Most will, and most will offer a special "startup package" or discount. Furthermore, you can attend local chamber of commerce events for free legal consulting sessions, which will most likely come with a promotional rate at the conclusion of the session.

Furthermore, accelerators, incubators, and co-working spaces almost always have free consultation sessions with lawyers as well as additional benefits and discounts. Remember, early-stage entrepreneurs need to be scrappy, creative, and need to turn over every rock to get every possible discount or free service they can.

How to save money: websites

Have you ever heard of Weebly, Wix, or Squarespace? These are the three simplest sites imaginable to put up a basic website. Remember, at this stage, even if your website can't do everything you want it to, it is more important to get one up.

With a basic website, you can put up information on your idea, set up a custom email address, put marketing materials up, and collect email addresses for an email list. Speaking of an email list, if all you need is a landing page or "coming soon" page, check out http://www.launchrock.com. It's an amazing tool for collecting early adopters' email addresses.

Remember, this is not designed to be your final website. This website is just meant to make you look more professional and to have a site that interested parties can visit. It will make you look more legit and you will get more respect when pitching it to potential partners, team members, and investors.

If you're a little bit more tech savvy, you can check out http://www.wordpress.com to make an even more functional website, though do note the slight learning curve.

How to save money: app development

Apps can get expensive real fast, especially if you're not a developer or educated on development. One of the best things you can do early on if you're planning on being an app or software entrepreneur is to take a basic crash course on development terms and methodologies. One really easy way to do this is to go to http://www.codeacademy.com and complete the "Ruby on Rails" module. This should only take you a few hours and will give you a very basic understanding as to what development is and what it actually takes. This will by no means make you an expert, but it will give you a basic understanding as to what your developers will be spending their time doing. If you're so intrigued, you can actually take two to three months to learn how to code for free and build your app for free instead of having to shell out $50,000 to other developers. Seriously think on that. Trust me, the six months it might take you to build will almost never eliminate your "first to market" advantage.

Alternatively, you can visit online learning sites like http://www.udemy.com or https://www.khanacademy.org and take a short intro class on coding. If your developers told you they will be building on PHP, Java, CSS and HTML, take intros to those languages so that you can at least speak the same language as they do. Doing this will also allow you to listen for those times when developers are trying to take advantage of you or rip you off.

You will be able to tell almost instantly if they're quoting you a fair price or overcharging you. (Most development firms grossly overcharge, and small-time developers will take advantage of inexperienced entrepreneurs.) Along with this strategy, you will want to employ the same tips from our general section. You will want to network as much as possible with developers and computer science experts. You will want to befriend a developer so that you can ask them if you are being ripped off. This person may also be able to connect you to good, local, reliable developers. This is a lot like having a good trusted family mechanic friend.

Don't make the mistake most first-time tech entrepreneurs make by offering a Chief Technology Officer role to the first developer they meet. You simply want to have this person as a friend. Yes, you may eventually hire him or her, but for now, we just need their advice to make sure we're not getting ripped off or overpaying for development work. Try buying them a beer for now before handing out a salary.

Now, before all of this, there is actually another well-kept secret that most first-time tech entrepreneurs don't know about. You don't need developers to make a prototype. What? How, you ask?

Wire framing.

Wire framing is the concept of first drawing your idea out on paper and then laying out screens for what your software or app will become. Check out http://www.balsamiq.com. You can use their software for free to create PDF mockups of what you want your app or website to become.

Wire framing serves two purposes. First, it allows you to clearly convey what you are trying to do visually to potential partners, team members, or investors. Second, it allows you to show

23

developers exactly what you want built. There will be no questions on goals or timelines because you are showing them exactly what you want them to build. This will always save you money with developers. Once you complete your Balsamiq wire frames, I recommend visiting https://www.invisionapp.com. Invision is an amazing tool that allows you to make a beautiful, fully clickable demo of your app or software. In order to do so, you will most likely want to work with some great UX/UI (user experience/user interface) designers as opposed to any old graphic designer. They will help you design your wire frames to be beautiful, and you can use this to presell software and raise money without shelling out development money!

Even though you will pay a premium for amazing Invision mockups, the total cost will be approximately $1/10^{th}$ of what actual development would cost!!!

If you're budgeting $100,000 to build your app, you can usually get amazing Invision mockups for $5,000 to $10,000! Now, instead of that scary

$100,000 you thought you needed to get started, you only need a fraction of that. Maybe you already have that money and can spend it on your dream instead of on some worthless material goods.

Trust me when I say this: You can use Invision mockups to raise money from both investors and potential clients. I have taken Invision mockups to trade shows before and secured over $50,000 in customer contracts without actually spending any money on development!

How to save money: market research

"Keep your cards close to your chest" is the exact wrong strategy to employ at this point. Let me be the first to tell you this very clearly. No one cares about your idea. In fact, you are literally about to embark on a journey where you are going to have to convince a great number of people to care about your idea. No one is going to steal your idea. They don't have the know-how, drive, passion or resources that you do. Trust me on this. I know it's hard to believe, but I guarantee you, no one is going to "steal" your idea. In fact, plenty of other people probably already have the idea. You just don't know about it. The temptation to use NDAs (non-disclosure agreements) at this stage is high but it serves as an immediate illustration as to your lack of experience as an entrepreneur. Your job at this stage is to spread the word. You need to be telling everyone about your idea. Not just close friends and family but people on the street, in the coffee shop, at the bar. You get the point. This is how you get free or very cheap early-stage market research. Try this. Sit in your local Starbucks and offer coffee to every person who walks through the door in exchange for answering a few questions about your idea. Within a few hours and for less than $100, you will have collected extremely valuable unbiased feedback. This feedback and overall talking to everyone about your idea, will allow you to recognize early flaws in your idea and also to identify new potential opportunities you may have overlooked.

If you choose to ignore this advice and play your cards close to your chest, the only thing you will be doing is protecting an idea from people who don't care about it. You'll end up spending thousands of dollars on some stupid market research firm when you could have collected direct customer feedback for the price of a few cups of coffee at Starbucks.

Finding creative and free ways to secure early and unbiased feedback helps to save money in your startup budget in two huge ways. First, as previously mentioned, you won't get sucked into the trap of paying a market research firm to validate your idea. You can eliminate the thousands of dollars that it would have cost you, and you can actually learn directly from potential customers early on. (Bonus Tip: Get their contact information and email them when you launch.) For more on this, be sure to read *The Lean Startup* by Eric Ries.

The second way that conducting market research in this way will help you save money on your startup budget is that you will identify very quickly which features, aspects, or offerings of your business are nice to have versus need to have. Allow me to explain.

All entrepreneurs, myself included, see the big picture of where our ideas can go. That's part of being an entrepreneur. Now, although this is a great and necessary quality, it creates a huge barrier to entry! What ends up happening is we take all of our ideas for the future and believe that they are all important. Perhaps down the line they will be, but for now you need potential customers to tell you which features or solutions they need. What immediate problem do you solve as simply as possible for them? Do you see where we are going here?

By conducting this early guerrilla style market research, you are getting direct unbiased feedback about which features/products/offerings customers will need versus just features you want. By taking this crucial, often overlooked step, you can cut 80% to 90% of the features you wanted in your software/business and save tens or even hundreds of thousands of dollars by cutting off features that are non-essential. Again, for more on this check out Ries' book.

How to save money: team members

One of the costliest aspects to any business is employees. They cost both time and money, and even worse, cofounders can also cost equity.

There is no perfect answer to how many cofounders you should have or how much the company should be split, but you should educate yourself on cap table management. For more on this, be sure to read *Founder's Pocket Guide: Cap Tables* by Stephen R. Poland.

One of the biggest mistakes first-time founders make is offering people cofounder status and equity far too early! Remember, the moment you make someone a cofounder, you marry them for the life of the business (through the good and the bad till death of the business do you part!).

Early on, the temptation is to jump at offering equity or cofounder status to people you think you need to succeed but this is almost always a terrible idea. If Elon Musk is offering to be a cofounder, give him whatever percent of your company he wants, but aside from that, let's take a step back.

The real key and trick to building a team early on for free or inexpensively is using what I call "trades and future promises." You are probably looking for cofounders or team members early on because they possess certain skills you don't have but need for your business to succeed.

Before we go any further, do not get sold or tricked into hiring or granting cofounder status to any sales or marketing "expert." You are being sold and will regret this decision later on. I have plenty of times. Let me be clear, I do not care how introverted or antisocial you are. You are responsible for sales and marketing until you have enough sales to hire someone for these roles.

Not only will this save you a ton of money on salaries, equity, and hard work, but doing the sales and marketing yourself early on gives you constant exposure to your potential customers so that you are constantly getting feedback, and if you're not closing deals, you will know why immediately. Anyway, back to our main points. You probably will need co-founders for your business. Ideally, these would be people who are already players in the industry: designers, developers, etc.

So how do you find these people and get them to work for you for free, for cheap, and or for no equity? Don't forget that you also have certain skills, connections, advice, experiences or goods that others may find valuable. The key here, much like everything else, in this phase is to be creative. If you need development work, try finding developers who hate their current jobs and who don't necessarily need more money but need the "light at the end of the tunnel" for their life. In other words, find people who want your startup to work out because they are not happy with their current jobs.

Oftentimes, you can approach these types of people, and you may find that this can be a way out for them. But don't have them quit their jobs because then you will have to pay them! Get them to work with you on a flex nights and weekends schedule. If you're not taking up too much of their time or pressuring them too hard, you can almost always get them to work for you for free for months just based on the future promise that they will receive some form of equity in the future (never throw out numbers).

The key thing to remember is that everything is negotiable, and you can make trades and creative offers if you know what to look for. If you are too lazy to do the work to find talent from the example above, your other option is interns! Interns are great because they usually just want experience or need college credit. Contrary to popular belief, you can almost always find high- quality interns who will work for free just to get experience, college credit, or the potential to work with you in the future. At this stage, you need   to lower your capital requirements as much as possible. Using these strategies to build a team early on will save you thousands and thousands of dollars now and even more in the future, as you will be vetting talent along the way.

Don't forget that there are a number of creative trades and future promises you can offer anyone, not just interns. Find talented people who have unique needs. Can you offer someone a place to stay in lieu of payment for work? Can you offer them a hot meal? A trade of services you can provide for them? Babysit for them for free on the weekends? This is the healthy and safe way to build a team and get work done for free or next to nothing early on. Get creative.

How to save money: miscellaneous

Overall, the goal here is to realize that you are trying to cut your budget as much as possible to conserve as much equity as possible as well as to minimize your risk and avoid any barriers to getting your idea off the ground. With this in mind, here are some other resources you can use to drastically cut down your startup costs (just Google them):

- Fiverr – Logos and more, a marketplace for just about anything entrepreneurs might need.
- UpWork – Hire freelancers to save money.
- LivePlan – Business plans and financial projections.
- Udemy – Learn to do anything.

- Code Academy – Learn to code.
- Meetup – Meet employees, investors, co-founders.
- WeWork – Find office space.
- Weebly/Wix/Squarespace – Get . . your website setup in under one hour.
- F6S – Find pitch competitions, accelerators, and incubators.
- Angel.co – Find investors and mentors.

PART II

HOW TO RAISE IT

The Basics

What this book is and what it is not

What this book all comes down to is that raising capital, just like entrepreneurship itself, is an art not a science. Contrary to popular belief or what VCs, the media, or Silicon Valley in general want you to believe, there is no roadmap to raising capital. As an entrepreneur, if you go down the path of being a fundraising founder—aka building a company that will require various capital injections in increasing amounts—you will find yourself meeting with dozens if not hundreds of individuals or interested groups. Some of these people and firms will fake interest just for entertainment, and others will actually be interested. Be careful and don't be afraid to "vet" the people or firms who claim they are interested in investing. A lot of the people and firms you meet will be extremely smart and potentially helpful in the future, but even more will be total phonies. Again, be careful.

This book is about securing early-stage capital through, ideally, you're first "round" or "first check." In the following sections, we're going to cover a number of creative and often overlooked ways of securing $500, $5,000, or even $50,000 in early-stage capital, some of which will require giving away no equity whatsoever! This book will define but will not cover a number of traditional ways of securing capital. We will define terms such as angel, seed, and venture capital. Sounds confusing? No worries. Following are the basic terms you should be aware of when raising money for your idea:

Definitions (for this book's sake):

- **First round capital** – The first round of outside money that is put into your startup. Note: the startup capital that you as the entrepreneur put in to incorporate the business or get a few logos/business cards is not your first round of capital.

- **First check** – The first outside investor check that comes into the company.

- **Equity** – Shares in your company that you distribute to investors partners in exchange for cash or services rendered.

- **Zero equity** – Deals that can be made without you having to give up any stake in your company.

- **Debt Financing -** Raising money through the use of funds which will have to be repaid either to an institution or individual at a later date.

- **Free money** – Funds that are received either as a gift or prize oftentimes in a competition. This kind of money has no repayment obligations and does not require you to give up any equity.

- **Grants** – Money made available to you either through the government or public institutions.

- **Crowdfunding** – A fairly new form of fundraising thanks to sites like Kickstarter and Indiegogo that allow companies and individuals to raise funds from individual, non-accredited investors through pre-sales/donations. This can be effective when executed properly.

- **Founder's Round** – A fundraising round where founders contribute capital to starting the business.

- **Friends and family round** – A friends and family round is essentially exactly what it sounds like. When you're just getting started you pitch your idea to close friends and family members to raise capital to get your idea off the ground. Their lack of experience with investing but faith in you often leads to an "easy" round of capital to secure but raising these kinds of funds comes with a lot of personal responsibility and a sense of moral obligation.

- **Super angels** – Investors who are willing to bet on you and your idea well before anyone else will. These investors will often commit capital on a very loose pitch just because they believe in you as an entrepreneur.

- **Angels** – Angels are typically your first outside investor. In other words, these people are not direct friends or family members. They are outside investors looking for a return on their money. These investors take on high risks by investing in companies early on and often expect a premium valuation for their money.

- **Seed round** – Usually referenced as the round where your first institutional money will come into the company.

- **Series A** – Often referenced as your first real fundraising round. Series A typically comes after a seed round and often requires your startup to have traction to secure real growth funding.

- **Series A2** – Not as common as a Series A, a Series A2 round is typically used to raise additional funds after a Series A either because the company needs those funds or there is a great deal of investor interest.

- **Series B** – Your first real round of pure growth capital. You need to show traction in some form in order to raise this round, and often times these funds can no longer be used loosely for development or marketing but rather must directly generate additional revenue, users, etc.

- **Series C** – Usually the last round of venture financing before an acquisition, a private equity investment or an IPO.

- **Series D/E** –Late-stage funding for companies that either want to stay private/ venture funded or have become so addicted to funding that they can't live without it until their company is acquired or dumped onto the public via an IPO.

- **IPO** – Initial Public Offering. The act of taking a company to the public for financing.

- **Private Equity** – Financingfromprofessional investors who are looking for solid growth business where their investments can turn a profit.

- **Accredited Investors** – In the U.S. accredited investors are individuals who have at least a net worth of $1,000,000 or an income of

- $200,000 for the last two years ($300,000 if married) and are expected to make the same this year.

- **JOBS act** – a fairly new law that allows for equity crowdsourcing. In essence it's a "mini-IPO."

- **Seed capital** – Funds contributed during a seed round of financing.

- **Pre-seed capital** – Funds contributed during a pre-seed round.

- **Pre-seed round** – Funds contributed by individual investors and sometimes institutions to help a company prepare for a seed round.

- **Rounds** – Shorthand term for fundraising rounds.

- **Bootstrapping** – Running a company as lean as possible without relying or even attempting to raise outside capital in most cases.

- **Incubator** – Programs that "incubate" companies and provide them with resources, connections, services, and a shared place to grow.

- **Accelerator** – Programs that typically invest funds into a company in exchange for equity and admission to a 3–18 month program that typically ends with a demo day.

- **Demo Day** – Final day of accelerator programs that gives startups an opportunity to pitch their companies to a pool of investors.

Finally, for additional clarity, here is the general order of funding rounds: Founder's Round // Friends and Family // Pre-Seed // Seed // Series A // Series A2 // Series B // Series C/D/E/F // Private Equity // IPO.

Now, let's dive in and take a look at how to raise your first round of capital.

Bootstrapping

Before you even think about taking in any outside money, you should seriously consider the cost of doing so because raising money actually has many costs associated with it—and not just financial ones either.

From debt to equity financing, every form of fundraising has some cost associated with it. Let's start with a basic and easy example to understand what I mean. Let's say you want to get a small business loan from your local bank that will come with interest or debt service payments. That means that even if you secure a loan for $10,000 you will end up paying back $12,500, an overall cost to you/your business of $2,500! Now, the reason that explains why these loans work is because the model is designed to give you time to get your business up and running before having to pay back that loan. But, if you talk to any seasoned entrepreneur, they will tell you that there is never a guarantee that your venture will work out, and then you can get behind on debt service payments, will have to file bankruptcy, make an additional bad deal (to stave off bankruptcy), or dig yourself into a deeper hole. Essentially, you're killing your business before it even has a chance to take off. Remember, a good rule of thumb is that in entrepreneurship everything takes at least three times longer to pan out than you think it will.

The same concept above applies to credit cards or a second mortgage on the house to an even more extreme degree. Trust me. I've made the mistake, and it almost killed me literally and has killed other entrepreneurs, not just their businesses. This is serious stuff, folks. This kills. Don't get fooled by the glamorous success stories. Airbnb's founders maxed out their credit cards, and consequently a survivorbiasemerges in the media—and then you're encouraged to believe that you can do the same and succeed. Stories like these, which also include budding entrepreneurs taking out an additional home mortgage or withdrawing funds from an account dedicated for a child's college tuition, are all glamorized as viable ways to get a business off the ground. Permit me to be honest: These are stupid things to do. Yes, entrepreneurship and ventures are risky, no question about it. But your goal at this stage is to get started for as little money as possible and to test to see if this is a venture that can make money.

These are the risks and costs associated with debt financing. Now, let's discuss equity financing. Most first-time entrepreneurs think equity financing is the solution to avoid all of the hassles, costs, and risks associated with debt financing. It is not.

Equity financing consists of giving away a percentage of your company to someone or a group in exchange for money that they put into the business. On the surface, this seems like a great no-cost option because they are "investing," and if you lose their money, it is what it is.

Let's review the first problem with this way of thinking. First off, equity financing is not free. Some of the financial costs associated with equity financing include travel to and from pitch meetings, costs associated with creating pitch decks, marketing materials, etc., and the cost of coffees/meals/entertainment for these meetings.

Don't think that all these things are inexpensive. Let's take a quick look at how fast things can add up.

Coffee for two ($10) x 20 meetings = $200
Dinner for two ($40) x 20 meetings = $800
Gas for Travel (six dollars) x 50 = $300
That's already over $1,000 for just local travel and a few meetings!

Considering how most entrepreneurs take 100+ meetings and travel across the country to raise equity funds, calculate how quickly that can add up to $10,000 or more before airfare!!!

Clearly, raising equity financing has fiscal costs associated with it, but let's cover the non-financial and often costlier reasons why equity financing is not free. Equity financing comes with partners, which is to say that new people can mess with the equilibrium of your new company. Anytime you give up equity in your company in exchange for money, you lose some of your independence. Sure, sometimes you get what's known as "smart money" or "strategic investors," but trust me, more often than not, at this stage, this is simply not the case. When you first start out in raising your first rounds of capital, anyone and everyone who bills themselves as an investor will be attractive. They may even tell you stories about how much they can help you and your company grow. Again, although it is possible to secure smart, strategic money early on, more often than not you're getting into bed with someone who is not as experienced or as skilled as he/she may want you to believe.

In these scenarios, what ends up happening is that you receive money in exchange for equity, and everything starts out rosy and great. You are pumped because you have your startup money and "experienced" investors on your team, and your investors are pumped because they think they are going to strike it rich with you. What happens from hereisyouenterwhatallexperiencedentrepreneurs will tell you is known as the "honeymoon" phase. For a period of six to 18 months you and this investor will get along great! You will have some awesome meetings, and because the first year of business is filled with more excitement than failure, you will be delivering mostly good news. After the honeymoon phase, though, these early investors will start getting a little more anxious and a little bit more involved. Increased number of phone calls, more requests for meetings, asking for financials, questioning your judgment and more. More often than not things will start to sour. You will begin to feel more pressure to ignore what you know is best and will have to listen to what these "experienced" (inexperienced) investors want you to do.

This is where the real cost of equity financing comes into play: mental, emotional, and physical stress. No matter how "good" your equity partners are, you cannot forget they are the money people. They invested because they want a return on their capital. Even if at the beginning they said they were in it for the long haul, they don't see your business or idea in the same light. When that honeymoon phase is over, that pressure alone can kill your business. Beware of equity capital.

Now, clearly, I am illustrating the worst possible cases for both debt and equity financing, but that is to illustrate the case for bootstrapping.

Bootstrapping is deciding early on that through the early stages of your business, you will not take on debt or equity partners but will rather be scrappy and use your own money, skills, and network to get started and build a solid foundation.

Bootstrapping is hard. It requires grit, tenacity, and creativity, but you will keep 100% equity in your business and will truly be your own boss.

Bootstrapping in business means using our "trades and future promises" strategies to get as much of your business up and running without having to take in outside money. Bootstrapping doesn't just save you from crushing debt or dangerous partners, but it has the added bonus of forcing you to learn each and every aspect of your business! When you finally reach the point where you are ready for growth capital, you will be able to pitch your business better because you will know the whole business inside and out and thus you will be able to command a higher valuation and can show investors that you are the real deal and can often dictate your own investment terms!

Now, bootstrapping doesn't mean you can't take in any money. You just have to take in the *right* money, or what I call "free money," and that's what we will cover next!

Free money

Most businesses/ ideas/ entrepreneurs don't need roughly 90% of the money they think they need to get started. If you think your website will cost $30,000 or even $3,000 you are likely not trying hard enough to cut down on your start up budget. Think long and hard about what we have already covered in this book. Really understand how much money you need to get started. The misconception we are trying to disprove here is the myth that your first round of capital needs to be enough to get you to compete with other firms. This is true only in very few instances. Your first rounds of capital are the bare minimum you need to get your idea off the ground, tested, hopefully validated, and increase the valuation of your startup the right way, but not through Silicon

Valley's financial engineering.

With this in mind, your first rounds of capital should ideally be a number between $500 and $50,000 (revisit the previous discussion on this). This chapter covers easy ways of securing either all of the capital or parts of it for free! No debt or equity financing! How is that possible? Through contests, accelerators, incubators and grants.

Contests

Let's start with contests: the enemy of the lazy entrepreneur. I meet with so many entrepreneurs on a day-to-day basis and have found in this modern age of entrepreneurship that many are not willing to do what it takes to be successful. This is a huge advantage for you as it means less competition when it comes to securing capital in ways that require a little elbow grease or critical thinking.

One approach is to join a contest. Do a quick search on the site called http://www.f6s.com and look at how many business plan/venture/pitch competitions are located in and around your city. Continue that search on Google and http://www.meetup.com and start looking at university competitions. Here is an example of a competition I helped found at the University of Central Florida, https://hospitality.ucf.edu/entrepreneur/.

Let's take this one step further. Have you heard of One Million Cups? Start by pitching there and getting plugged into your local entrepreneurship community. Ask about upcoming pitch competitions and what it takes to enter.

Competitions are amazing. They are stressful, nerve-racking, and fill you with fear. It's great practice for feelings you will have for the rest of your life as an entrepreneur, but they also serve as great practice for getting over these fears.

Even if a contest has no prize money associated with it, you are getting "free money" in the form of feedback, free press, and potential connections to investors, team members, and clients in the audience.

Now, I know what you are thinking. "Julien, screw you. This isn't free money! I need cold hard cash!" Not to worry. The truth is that most of these competitions, including the one I founded, offer prize money in varying amounts. Most offer first-, second-, and third-place prizes with prize pools ranging from $500 - $500,000!! Think about that! Instead of wasting the next three months pitching friends, family, or angels for $50,000, why not enter 10+ competitions and get fully funded by winning just one or two? Best part is you don't have to give up any equity in your company! Seriously, consider this as a viable option to fund your business. Compile 10, 20, 30, 50+ competitions that you can attend and start submitting applications. Plan to do a pitching circuit and set up additional meetings when you travel to these competitions. Here are a few resources to do this efficiently:

- F6S - http://www.f6s.com
- AngelList – http://www.angel.co
- CrunchBase – http://www.crunchbase.com
- Meetup – http://www.meetup.com

Accelerators and Incubators

Accelerators and incubators are amazing programs when done properly. Unfortunately, in today's entrepreneurial environment, there are many bad accelerators and incubators out there, but if you can find a good one, you can easily get $100,000 or more in (semi-free) money (more on this in a moment).

What are accelerators and incubators? These are programs designed to help entrepreneurs in the earliest stages of their businesses to get them off the ground. They consist (the good ones at least) of a network of entrepreneurs, investors, advisors, mentors, lawyers, and any other number of services that you may need to get your business up and running. In addition, many of these programs award money for getting into their program in exchange for a small percentage in your company. Be careful. Make sure that the accelerator is legitimate and well known, and you should never really be asked to give up more than roughly 7% to these programs.

If you're working with a well-known accelerator, this can be one of the best decisions you'll ever make, as they now have a small stake in your company and will (should) do everything in their power to help you succeed. Analyze which accelerators are a best fit for you and start applying.

Incubators are slightly different from accelerators. Accelerators tend to be three-month programs that are designed (at least in theory) to help you reach scale quickly. They tend to be more involved with your startup, offer you a temporary office space, and usually conclude with a demo day (a pitch exhibition where you can secure additional funding).

On the other hand, incubators tend to be less involved yet are more long-term. Many are government funded and are programs/facilities designed to give you a hub in which to let your business blossom. Incubators don't always come with capital and investment but they do come with free or subsidized office space and common areas to network with other entrepreneurs, mentors/ advisors, and they often offer discounts on any number of business services. In addition, incubators often host helpful workshops and seminars aimed at getting your business off the ground. Use the same resources from the section above to research incubators which may be a fit for you.

Grants

Often overlooked, grants, scholarships, and other government funding options do exist for startups. Due to their limited nature of availability we will not cover different kinds of grants in this book, but you can do additional research as you see fit.

Self-funding

Put your money where your mouth is (just don't bet the house or the kids' college fund). The easiest, safest, and honestly best way to get started on any project is to contribute the first round of capital yourself. It is low risk and shows future investors you are not just an "idea person" but that you've put skin in the game. This is why our earlier exercise (saving money) was so important.

When it comes to self-funding, you don't need to dish out $300,000. You can start with $1,500 to get your site up, get your LLC filed, and get some business cards made! For as little as $1,500 you will not only look and feel like a business owner, you will be one! The key here is to strategically deploy your own money on the one or two most important items that constitute the bare minimum to get your idea off the ground. The misconception around self-funding is that you have to be independently wealthy to do so. This could not be further from the truth. Entrepreneurs—that, is, real entrepreneurs— are hustlers. When our backs are against the wall, we find a way to break down that wall. Nothing is impossible to a real entrepreneur. Let's start here. We all have problems. A sick mother you have to take care of. A job you hate. Bad relationships. Kids to support. Whatever. These are all serious issues, but are you going to use them as excuses to not chase your dreams. Most people do. Entrepreneurs don't. We find a way. We sleep three hours at night and work three jobs for nine months to put money aside to self-fund our projects. We sacrifice friendships, relationships, material goods, vacations, health (not recommended) and any number of other things that most people don't see because they don't want to see it. We all have the same 24 hours in a day, and we all have problems. If you want this bad enough, you can always find a way to make it work. Anything less is an excuse. With this in mind, let's get into some self-funding strategies.

Nights and weekends

What do you do before or after work? Do you veg out for a bit? Watch Netflix? Hang with friends? Cook? Give that up. Either work on your startup or get a second or third job for a few months to save up the money you need to get a prototype made. Same goes for weekends. Thanks to social media, people think being an entrepreneur is glamorous. It is not.

All of us—and that includes me as I was writing this book—worked nights (10 pm to 3 am) and weekends to get our projects off the ground. Don't let fake entrepreneurs on Instagram let you believe otherwise. We sacrifice. We hustle. We struggle and we fight. We do whatever it takes to make it, and when that's not enough, and we fail, we keep going and do it all over again. Don't kid yourself. This book isn't designed to lie to you and to motivate you to "start." It's designed to be a ray of common sense in a convoluted entrepreneurial ecosystem. Sacrifice and entrepreneurship go hand in hand. This is a very lonely game, and if you don't feel that way at least sometimes throughout the process, you're not playing it right.

Self-funding is a sacrifice. It requires you to work more. Alienate friends. Put relationships or having a family on hold, but in the end, it is 100% worth it. If you can sacrifice nights, weekends, and sleep, you can and will find a way to bring in extra income to fund your project.

This is a hard pill for many to swallow, but it is the truth. With all of this being said, the trick to self-funding is to find or create a situation which makes it easier to secure these funds. Remember, entrepreneurs need to be creative. So, when we say get a second or third job, it doesn't immediately mean bussing tables part time. What skills do you possess? Can you freelance on a site like http://

www.upwork.com or http://www.fiverr.com to supplement that additional income? Freelancing on sites like these, allows you to generate additional money all from home while in your pajamas. What about your network? Any friends, parents, relatives who are business owners? Reach out to them and see if they have any extra work you can help with (we almost always do and are happy to help out another entrepreneur). Get creative, folks. This can be as easy or as difficult as you make it, just don't ever complain and whine about it. This is the life you chose. The life we all chose.

How about local weekend jobs in your community? Can you help out at the local farmers market? Read to children at the local library? Tutor? Teach guitar lessons? This is all about hustling, folks! Get that through your head. You have to do what it takes to realize your dream no matter how difficult or impossible it may seem right now.

Let's take this whole job thing a step further. Let's say you're a piano player and have a business idea for a new electric piano or even a new software to help teach piano. Instead of going to work at McDonald's for that extra money you need to self-fund the project, why not start teaching piano lessons at night and on the weekends so that you are earning money while field testing your idea! This works in almost every situation. New idea for hotels, go work there and learn the processes to see if it would work. Idea for a restaurant? Same thing. Idea for machine learning? Freelance. The principle is the same across the board. Maximize how you spend your time to gain relevant knowledge and feedback while at the same time self-funding your business. Think smarter, not harder. Get creative and find a way. Don't be a whiny, complaining fake entrepreneur and by saying things like "I'm too busy," "I'm too stressed," or "I have too much going on." Get off your high horse and get to work.

Craigslist, eBay, Letgo

Now, remember that the goal here with self-funding is to get the minimum amount of money required to get your business going. You might actually have this money lying around in your house! What? How? The trick is to realize that this money may not necessarily be visible in the form of cold hard cash... yet.

Craigslist, eBay, Letgo, and even a plain ol' garage sale can be your best friend(s) when it comes to self-funding a business or project. Start checking the attic, the basement, the storage unit, the junk drawer or the shoebox in the back of the closet. Do you really need those new Jordan's? What about that old iPod/iPhone? All those clothes? (Check out Plato's Closet.) How about that snowboard from that one time you went snowboarding years ago and "were going to get all into it"? How about that Rolex? Yeah, it might be tough to let go, but sell them. Obviously, a family heirloom you may want to keep, but think about all of the hidden money you are sitting on by holding on to these things. It may suck to let go now, but what would suck more is spending your whole life miserable working for someone else wondering "what if" and never chasing your dreams.

Even though it may suck to sell your things on eBay, think about the potential you have once you have your startup capital. If your business takes off, you can buy an Audemars Piquet instead of that Rolex you sold. That snowboard you hated parting with? Now you can fly private with friends to Vail and actually get the lessons you need to crush it on the mountain. Practice reframing situations like this all the time. It's one of the most important skills you can develop as an entrepreneur. I highly recommend reading Oren Klaff's book, *Pitch Anything!* to truly understand framing situations.

Clearly, self-funding has many different approaches, but the goal here is to realize that it is possible to find, save, or generate the $500 to $50,000 personally that you would need to get started.

Isn't it easier just to raise that money and get started now? Remember, debt and equity financing are not free and come with partners and investors who can cause crazy amounts of stress. You will also appreciate your startup money and allocate your capital in a smarter, more frugal manner since you had to work for it. Weigh your own personal pros and cons of self-funding and make an informed decision. And remember this: After you have your garage sale, or sell stuff on eBay, or whatever it is you decide to do to raise money, always set up a separate bank account to save funds!

Founder's Round(s)

Starting a business with multiple founders? Much like self-funding, a founder's round consists of all founding members contributing capital to get the business started. This is a great way to get operations funded quickly for a fraction of the price of self-funding.

Think of a founder's round in the same way you'd think of splitting cab fare. You and your buddies are planning for a night out. You can Uber downtown yourself for $60 or can walk to their house and split a cab four ways ($15 as opposed to $60). Now, this saves you money, but as anyone who has ever done this can tell you, you lose freedom, comfort, and autonomy in exchange for that $45 savings. Someone may be taking forever to get ready and now you're not getting to the bar or party until 1 am instead of 11 pm. The Uber can get crowded (a freeloader can jump in and be the fifth person in a four-person car). We all know this happens! Someone might poke you. Someone may get into a fight over who sits where. Maybe there's a fight if you spill that "to go" cup on a friend when the Uber goes over a pothole. Maybe someone gets sick on the way, and you have to turn around and never make it to the party. Maybe the people you are "splitting" with conveniently don't have an updated Uber app when it is time to split the cost. Think about everything you have sacrificed to save that $45. This is what happens in founder's rounds. They are great if everything goes "smoothly" or according to plan, but there are countless opportunities for things to go wrong.

Friends, Family—and Fools

This is the most common form of raising early stage startup capital. We won't spend too much time on the actual process of securing capital from these types of individuals, as the process is actually rather simple: have idea, talk to friends/family, get the check for $2,000. Seriously, it's really that easy. But easy doesn't always mean good! Money from friends and family is oftentimes easy to secure but also some of the most stressful to use. Losing mom and dad's hard-earned money sucks. Losing that money your best friend put in sucks. Losing your cousin's money who trusted you with $5,000 sucks. It is painful, stressful, and downright scary. This being said, if done properly, securing friends' and family money can be a viable way to get started. The key here starts with your pitch: "You will probably lose this money. Are you okay with that?" Use that line on everyone in this round. This is not the time and these are not the people you want to "sell." You want them to invest what they can (disposable income) in you because they are a friend or family member, and they want to support you! The beauty with friends and family money is that you can oftentimes secure a check for a tiny promise of equity or for a 0% interest loan. Think smart and do your research here. Be fair, but don't be over generous with doling out equity at this stage to these people.

Even though they love you, this is not experienced money. It's just money. Weigh the cost/benefit of going down this route as opposed to self-funding and seriously learn about capitalization tables before liberally dishing out equity. Remember, you don't want to siphon as much money as you can out of these people. You want stress-free money, money that these people are comfortable losing. Remember that!

A note on friends' and family money. Most first-time founders assume that money from friends and family is limited to your "friends and family". This couldn't be further from the truth. What money from friends and family means is going through your extended network of friends and family and seeing who a strategic investor might be. This is where the real power comes from with friends' and family money. Experienced founders know how to do these searches on LinkedIn and to strategically ask friends and family members for introductions. Once again, get creative!

Customer Financing

Hands down this is the single best way to finance a company that we will cover in this book. That being said, it is also the most difficult, as are most things in life that are worth pursuing.

Customer financing revolves around just that: pre-selling or flat out selling subscriptions to your service or units of your product to finance your operations. Let's take a look at an example as to when this might be possible. Let's say you're a developer and can code your whole app by yourself. What you would do is build it on your own without having to shell out any startup capital and then release it in the app store, get some early ad dollars or sales, and wait to hire team members or do any expansion until you secure that money. You literally use customer revenues to build your business. Another example of when this would be possible is by pre-selling a contract. Let's say you had come up with a new way to produce oil from grass (let me know if you have; I will invest). What you would do is start bidding on contracts to supply oil to companies who have demand for it. So, prior to building your refineries, hiring hundreds of people, etc., you bid on the contract, hopefully win, and then use the advanced payments on that contract on financing to get up and running. Sounds complicated and hectic? That's because it is. Welcome to entrepreneurship.

Now, obviously these are both extreme examples, but the principles are sound. Find a way to get someone to pay for or buy your goods or services before actually producing them and you will successfully finance your company without ever having to give up any equity! Worth thinking about!

Crowdfunding

A relatively new way of funding companies is crowdfunding. I helped write a curriculum for a crowdfunding course at Rollins College, and have advised several clients on crowdfunding and will most likely use crowdfunding in some way for the launch of this book.

Crowdfunding is a democratized, creative form of fundraising. What most people don't realize is that generally when you raise funds for a startup you usually have to raise from accredited investors. Crowdfunding makes it possible to raise money from every day folks including your friends and family, potential clients, and even social media followers. By using a popular site such as Kickstarter or Indiegogo, you can easily set up a campaign and start raising funds immediately.

Before doing so, I highly recommend taking an e-course on crowdfunding, as it is not as simple as it is made out to be. Crowdfunding is not guaranteed in that you usually must set a target for your fundraise, and if you don't hit that target, you keep zero dollars. Successful crowdfunding campaigns require careful planning, marketing and cash reserves in case you don't meet your goal.

Do your research here as well. Crowdfunding takes time and diligent management. Additionally, crowdfunding isn't right for every type of project. Make sure your project fits into a category, find other successful projects that are similar to yours, and do what they did.

JOBS Act

The rise of crowdfunding has led to a new type of funding, which is slowly becoming known as equity crowdfunding. The JOBS Act (Jumpstart Our Business Startups Act) has opened up a whole new way for companies to get funded.

Please do research on this and see if it is right for you.

Angels and Super Angels

Angels and Super Angels are people who make investments, mostly individual, sometimes through a group or "syndicates," in very early stage risky ventures.

Let's start here. Not all angels are created equal! First off, angels can be your best or worst investors, so it's important you understand what makes a good angel investor. Most angel investors will cut checks between $25,000 and $250,000 for an equity stake in your company (hopefully between 4% to 12%), but just because they have the money, does not mean you should take it.

Angels who have made their money in brick and mortar businesses, for example, will not necessarily be a great fit to most tech startups. Furthermore, former tech entrepreneurs may not be the right fit to invest in a new beverage company. You need to take this into account.

Remember, up until this point, we have covered how you can source anywhere between

$500–$50,000 on your own without giving up equity. That means, if you were considering giving up equity for a $25,000 check, this angel better damn well be worth it! Let's pause and reframe   a common narrative the entrepreneur must continuously overcome. People with money don't necessarily have all the power. That's what they want you to believe, and that's why many can be rude, arrogant, and condescending. It's a power trick aimed at devaluing you and putting a high importance on their checkbook thus securing them a better deal. Just remember, in this situation, in this game and in life in general, people only have as much power over you as you allow them to.

So, how do we tell if we're dealing with a good angel or not? Vet them. Don't take every single meeting. Many "angels" today are just bored, retired folks who want to use their false promise of money to you as a way to get a night out of the house and some entertainment. Don't get duped. Has this angel invested before? Have other founders had positive or negative experiences with them? Are they really successful founders or did they spend 30 years at IBM? I cannot stress how important it is to vet investors. Do not skip this step!

Now that that's out of the way, how do you find angels? What we want to look for here is an independently wealthy individual with prior experience in the field you want to break into and who has a personality you can get along with. This person will most likely be and should be the most active investor in your company.

I can't stress this enough: All things considered, make sure the two of you get along and that you both have the same general strategic vision for the company! Don't try to impress this person, don't change who you are, don't lie about how far along you are, and don't change your vision of the company to conform to their views. With angels and any other investor, never be afraid to walk away from the table. No amount of money is worth working with someone who has a different vision for the company. This is the heart attack (silent killer) of so many young companies.

So, if this is the case and we have already covered how to secure $500 - $50,000 in "free money," why even bother with angels? Well, angels are a super-important part of your company. Imagine having someone like Jason Calacanis invest in your company. Don't know who he is? Look him up. He's probably the most famous angel of modern times, not to mention one of the best.

If you do your homework properly, you should be able to find a very strategic angel who will not only invest in your company but will help it rocket to the next level by opening up their network and industry connections and even customers to you. Furthermore, an angel such as Calacanis can play a huge role in helping you secure future rounds of funding from VCs and institutions. Find great angels, and they will carry you to heaven on their wings. Find bad angels and they will drag you down with them.

A quick note on super angels. Super angels are investors who usually cut check sizes for $25,000 or less whereas angels are generally $25,000–$250,000. I cannot say this enough: Make sure that you vet these people and that you also get along with them. You might think that finding someone with less money (less than $25,000) means less risk or that you won't be getting in bed with a bad angel. Not true. In fact, more often than not, smaller, inexperienced investors with more to lose will cause you more stress down the line.

We have now reached a crucial point in this book. Angels are about as far as we will go with regards to the "how you can get the money" section. Remember, this book is really about helping you raise that first $500 - $50,000 and already with angels we are approaching the

$25,000 - $250,000 range in exchange for a larger portion of equity. Angels and beyond will require pitch decks, financial projections, term sheets, and more headaches, Venture Capitalists will want to see some form of traction or a prominent team/ background to really secure the best kind of funding in these rounds. Let me be clear. Thanks to modern-day Silicon Valley, you can skip straight to angel rounds or beyond with just an idea, but this book is about explaining why that's not always a great idea and how instead you can secure the capital you need to get started much more easily, with less stress—and sometimes for free.

In this book we will not cover additional fundraising options and types of investors, but these options (including angels) should only be entertained after you secure your first $500 - $50,000 through the aforementioned methods to get your business off the ground, validated, and running. You want to build a good foundation first. If you don't, and you play the SV fundraising game of "let's just raise $1mm at 10% and get our startup valued at $10mm right away," you will be at the mercy of that game and investors for the entire lifetime of the company.

I wrote this book to show you that you don't have to play that game. You can secure funds to get up and running and then dictate your own investment terms instead of losing all your power to investors. Please take the creative methods of raising early stage capital outlined in this book very seriously. They can save you from many pitfalls.

Optional Contract

I,_____, promise to be a responsible founder and will review the exercises in this book over and over until I determine the amount of money I need to get started. Then and only then will I decide which method for raising my first round of capital I will use.

Sign: _____

The Bottom Line

In the end, this book was written to show you that early-stage capital is actually much easier to secure than you might have previously thought. The goal of this book is to reframe and redefine what early-stage capital actually means. As we have mentioned so many times throughout this book, startup money (early-stage capital) is and always will be out there, but not all money is created equal. We covered strategies to really determine how much startup capital you need and then outlined creative ways to actually secure those funds.

The big thing to remember here is that modern-day VCs want you to believe that their way of raising money and building companies with stupid high valuations is the only way to play the game. As we have explored and exposed in this book, it is not, especially when you finally wake up and understand that early-stage capital really does mean securing that first $500 - $50,000 to get up and running.

In fact, this book was written because having personally played the VC financing game, I believe that today's form of entrepreneurship and financing of companies simply cannot last. Startups, specifically tech startups, are due for a market correction at some point very soon (for more on this, listen to my podcast at *www.SFNSHOW.com*). With all this in mind, my goal has been to put together a guide to help my fellow entrepreneurs redefine and reimagine what it takes to get funded. I hope you agree that First Money In has been helpful for you as you work toward reaching your goals. If you get nothing else out of this book, just remember to always consider the pros and cons of raising any kind of money. Not all money and not all investors are created equal!

And so with that, good luck to entrepreneurs everywhere!

Sincerely,
Julien Louis Meyer, MBA
Entrepreneur and Host of Startup Financial News

Glossary (Compile all Terms)

- **First round capital** – The first round of outside money that is put into your startup. Note: the startup capital that you as the entrepreneur put in to incorporate the business or get a few logos/business cards is *not* your first round of capital.

- **First check** – The first outside investor check that comes into the company.

- **Equity** – Shares in your company that you distribute to investors or partners in exchange for cash or services rendered.

- **Zero equity** – Deals that can be made

without you having to give up any stake in your company.

- **Debt financing** – Raising money through the use of funds which will have to be repaid either to an institution or individual at a later date.

- **Free money** – Funds that are received either as a gift or prize oftentimes in a competition. This kind of money has *no* repayment obligations and does *not* require you to give up any equity.

- **Grants** – Money made available to you either through the government or public institutions.

- **Crowdfunding** – A fairly new form of fundraising thanks to sites like Kickstarter and Indiegogo that allow companies and individuals to raise funds from individual, non-accredited investors through pre-sales/donations. This can be effective when executed properly.

- **Founder's Round** – A fundraising round where founders contribute capital to starting the business.

- **Friends and family round** – A friends and family round is essentially exactly what it sounds like. When you're just getting started you pitch your idea to close friends and family members to raise capital to get your idea off the ground. Their lack of experience with investing but faith in you often leads to an "easy" round of capital to secure but raising these kinds of funds comes with a lot of personal responsibility and a sense of moral obligation.

- **Super angels** – Investors who are willing to bet on you and your idea well before anyone else will. These investors will often commit capital on a very loose pitch just because they believe in you as an entrepreneur.

- **Angels** – Angels are typically your first outside investor. In other words, these people are not direct friends or family members. They are outside investors looking for a return on their money. These investors take on high risks by investing in companies early on and often expect a premium valuation for their money.

- **Seed round** – Usually referenced as the round where your first institutional money will come into the company.

- **Series A** – Often referenced as your first real fundraising round. Series A typically comes after a seed round and often requires your startup to have traction to secure real growth funding.

- **Series A2** – Not as common as a Series A, a Series A2 round is typically used to raise additional funds after a Series A either because the company needs those funds or there is a great deal of investor interest.

- **Series B** – Your first real round of pure growth capital. You need to show traction in some form in order to raise this round, and often times these funds can no longer be used loosely for development or marketing but rather must directly generate additional revenue, users, etc.

- **Series C** – Usually the last round of venture financing before an acquisition, a private equity investment or an IPO.

- **Series D/E** – Late-stage funding for companies that either want to stay private/ venture funded or have become so addicted to funding that they can't live without it until their company is acquired or dumped onto the public via an IPO.

- **IPO** – Initial Public Offering. The act of taking a company to the public for financing.

- **Private Equity** – Financing from professional investors who are looking for solid growth business where their investments can turn a profit.

- **Accredited Investors** – In the U.S. accredited investors are individuals who have at least a net worth of $1,000,000 or an income of

- $200,000 for the last two years ($300,000 if married) and are expected to make the same this year.

- **JOBS act** – a fairly new law that allows

for equity crowdsourcing. In essence it's a "mini-IPO."

- **Seed capital** – Funds contributed during a seed round of financing.

- **Pre-seed capital** – Funds contributed during a pre-seed round.

- **Pre-seed round** – Funds contributed by individual investors and sometimes institutions to help a company prepare for a seed round.

- **Rounds** – Shorthand term for fundraising rounds.

- **Bootstrapping** – Running a company as lean as possible without relying or even attempting to raise outside capital in most cases.

- **Incubator** – Programs that "incubate" companies and provide them with resources, connections, services, and a shared place to grow.

- **Accelerator** – Programs that typically invest funds into a company in exchange for equity and admission to a 3 - 18 month program that typically ends with a demo day.

- **Demo Day** – Final day of accelerator programs that gives startups an opportunity to pitch their companies to a pool of investors.

Resources Mentioned in this Book

Links

Meet People - http://www.meetup.com Legal Advice - http://www.nolo.com

Learn Online - https://www.udemy.com/how-to-start-a-startup-business/

Learn Online - https://www.khanacademy

Put up a Landing Page - http://www.launchrock.com Put up a website - http://www.wordpress.com

Put up a website – http://www.weebly.com Learn to Code - http://www.codeacademy.com Wireframes - http://www.balsamiq.com Wireframes - https://www.invisionapp.com

Find Accelerators & Incubators - http://www.f6s.com

Julien's Pitch Competition - https://hospitality.ucf.edu/entrepreneur/

Find Investors, Accelerators & Incubators - http://www.angel.co

Find Investors - http://www.crunchbase.com Find
Talent - http://www.upwork.com

Find Talent - http://www.fiverr.com

Books

Never Split the Difference: Negotiating As If
Your Life Depended On It by Chris Voss

The Lean Startup by Eric Ries

Founder's Pocket Guide: Cap Tables by
Stephen R. Poland

Disrupt You! by Jay Samit Pitch Anything! by
Oren Klaff

Managing Oneself by Peter F. Drucker

About the Author

Julien Meyer got his start as an entrepreneur very young and has been a career entrepreneur ever since. In the 4th grade he hosted a lunchtime bartering station at his desk; in the 6th grade he sold bubble gum at his middle school; and in his high school years he sold a plethora of products, including skateboards and cell phones, to other students. In his early college days, Meyer started a nightlife event-service company that provided DJs, bartenders, security guards, and party planners to his clients. Meyer has since gone on to run multiple startups as founder and CEO of collegeTKTS, CollegeStack, and BlurtBox, and is now the lead startup coach and chief VC consultant at the NYC-based firm MGI Capital.

Julien Meyer has been featured in a number of publications, including *Small Business Today, UCF Today, Central Florida Future*, and is a UCF Order of Pegasus Recipient. Mr. Meyer is a graduate of the University of Central Florida, and has an MBA from Rollins College. He is currently the host of the popular Startup Financial News, a daily news podcast for Apple's iTunes platform, where you can hear his daily take on entrepreneurial current events.

With Special Thanks

This book was made possible by the hard work of so many people and it would be impossible to thank all parties. If you have been a supporter, you know who you are and my infinite thanks are extended to you all.

With that being said, I would like to especially thank God, my family and friends who all made this book a reality. This book would not have been possible without the tireless work of my loving mother, Lisa Meyer. Without the love and support of my father Paul Meyer, brothers Franck and Frankie, and of course my entire extended family.

I would also like to especially thank Barry Lyons, my wonderful editor, whose encouraging words and knowledgeable editing insight, brought this book to fruition.

I would also like to extend a special thank you to *Arthur "Artie" Stoeke, Julian Correa, Caleb Edwards, Craig Bolz, Kristen Wiley, Jason Calacanis, Oren Klaff, Jay Samit, Chris Voss, Sergie Albino,*

Brian Ross, Terrance Berland, David Scalzo, David Pearl, Cameron Brown, Alexander Kontos, Chris Harrison, the entire BlurtBox team, Alfredo Castro, Brendan Blake, Phil Brady, the Battiato family, Matthew Ockwell, Steven Tom, Bonnie Halper, Luke Attebery, Saeed Jabbar, Joe Merlino, Ryan Burke, Tres Loch, Gio Borges, Anthony Mawyin, Nathan & Shawn, Andres Correa, all of my MGI clients, UCF, Rollins College, Greg Speleotes, Andrew Amaro, Emily Karson, Tom Jimenez, Dominique Godefroy, Sadaf Mackertich, Dennis Levy, Jeff Weinland, Jason Sarkoyan, and finally P1design Group for the amazing layout and formatting of this book and cover.

This book has all been made possible through all of your inspiration and support. Thank you.

Notes

Always Remember

"You're only nobody, until the day
that you're somebody."

Julien Louis Meyer

www.ingramcontent.com/pod-product-compliance
Lightning Source LLC
Chambersburg PA
CBHW070129240526
45468CB00002BA/564